UNDER T... WHALEBACK

Richard Bean

UNDER THE WHALEBACK

OBERON BOOKS
LONDON

WWW.OBERONBOOKS.COM

First published in 2003 by Oberon Books Ltd
521 Caledonian Road, London N7 9RH
Tel: +44 (0) 20 7607 3637 / Fax: +44 (0) 20 7607 3629
e-mail: info@oberonbooks.com
www.oberonbooks.com

A catalogue record for this book is available from the British
Library.

PB ISBN: 978-1-84002-286-5
E ISBN: 978-1-84943-157-6

Visit www.oberonbooks.com to read more about all our books
and to buy them. You will also find features, author interviews and
news of any author events, and you can sign up for e-newsletters
so that you're always first to hear about our new releases.

ACKNOWLEDGEMENTS

I'd like to thank Gordon Grindley, Paul Miller, Chris Campbell, Rose Cobbe, Dinah Wood, Ian Rickswon, Graham Whybrow, Richard Wilson, Laurence Mitchell, Ken Collier, Jim Williams, the crew of the Artic Corsair, Alf Hodson and all the staff at National Fishing Heritage Museum.

Characters

The Kingston Jet

CASSIDY

a deckhand, aged fifty-five

DARREL

a deckie learner aged seventeen

The James Joyce

DARREL

a deckhand, aged twenty-four

NORMAN

a deckhand, aged twenty-eight

ROC

a deckhand, aged thirty-one

BAGNALL

the third hand, aged thirty-six

BILL

a deckhand, aged fifty-five

The Arctic Kestrel

DARREL

fifty-four

(*to be played by Cassidy from Act One*)

PAT

twenty-nine

(*to be played by Norman from Act Two*)

ELLY

nine

Set

The crew's quarters in the forecastle, under the
whaleback of a 1950s-built 800-ton sidewinder
trawler. Eight bunks are arranged on two tiers,
stage left being the starboard side and stage right
the port side. The bunks are made of varnished
plywood. Each has a curtain which can be
drawn across. Centre stage is a table fixed to the
floor and around it, and again fixed and built
in, are upholstered benches. There are tell-tale
differences for each ship but the basic structure
is the same.

Under the Whaleback was first performed at the Royal Court Theatre Upstairs on 10 April 2003, with the following cast:

The Kingston Jet

DARREL, Iain McKee

CASSIDY, Alan Williams

The James Joyce

DARREL, Iain McKee

NORMAN, Matthew Dunster

ROC, Richard Stacey

BAGNALL, Ian Mercer

BILL, Sam Kelly

The Arctic Kestrel

DARREL, Alan Williams

PAT, Matthew Dunster

ELLY, Sophie Bleasdale

Director, Richard Wilson

Designer, Julian McGowan

Lighting Designer, Johanna Town

Sound Designer, Gareth Fry

Casting, Lisa Makin

The Kingston Jet

1965. The forecastle of the Kingston Jet. On the bulwark is a large black and white centrefold pin-up. The ship is in dock and there is a slight list to port. The sound of a ship's horn off. A different ship's horn replies, long and mournful, a different note. A third horn, very deep, joins in. Pause. The first horn sounds again in two short blasts. The second horn sounds in one short blast. Pause. The third horn sounds deep, long, and mournful. Voices off.

CASSIDY: (*Off.*) Eh Ray! Where we going?! Where yer tekking us this time yer shitehawk?!

RAY: (*Off.*) Mind yer own fucking business Cassidy!

CASSIDY: (*Off.*) Godshaven! Greenland! Get mesen a nice little tight arsed Eskimo. Show this lad the northern lights! Ha, ha!

RAY (*Off.*) Where's that dog of yours?

CASSIDY: (*Off.*) She's not coming this trip.

RAY: (*Off.*) No dog?!

CASSIDY: (*Off.*) No dog! No fucking wuff, wuff, wuff!

RAY: (*Off.*) Get yersen under that whaleback Cass, yer pissed.

CASSIDY: (*Off.*) Gerroff me Ray!

RAY: (*Off.*) Alright! Eh, Snacker, give him hand down that companionway.

(CASSIDY falls down the companionway with a crash.)

(*Off.*) You alright Cass!

CASSIDY (*Off.*) Yeah! I'm dead!

DARREL: (*Off.*) He's alright sir.

(Enter CASSIDY holding a tube design kit bag, sea boots, and a mattress. He is a 55 year old man. He wears a suit and a lemon coloured shirt, the collar of which is over the lapels of his jacket. The shirt and cuffs are covered in blood. He is drunk.)

CASSIDY Dead! And gone to a better place. Ha, ha!

(Enter DARREL. He is 17 and dressed in the fashions of the day. He has the same gear as CASSIDY, but his is brand new.)

DARREL: 'Ave you hurt yersen?

CASSIDY: Banged me fucking head dint I.

DARREL: You're bleeding.

CASSIDY: Aye! Look son, you can call me dad. Father and son. Wa, they'll all tek the piss, but let them I say, you can't break the bond of blood, blood is thicker than water. Call me 'dad'. And I'll call you – 'son'. Don't call me daddy.

DARREL: I'd prefer Darrel, or Daz. Me mates call me Daz.

CASSIDY: Blood! Blood's different. I'll call you son. And I'll learn yer all I know about fishing. Distant water. Right, for starters, them stairs out there, them int stairs, alright? – that's fishing for yer, and ships, everything's gorra different name. 'Companionway.' Remember it by thinking of yer 'companions' using it as the 'way' – down or up. Now, the right way to come down a companionway is facing the steps with yer toes in the gaps.

(He mimes it.)

If yer try and come down facing forrard, forward, forrard, yeah? Yer wimme?

DARREL: Forrard.

CASSIDY – you'll likely as not go arse over tit.

DARREL: Like you did.

CASSIDY: Brilliant! That's my boy. Two. If yer carrying owt, carry it in one hand only, and leave one hand to hang on with. 'One hand for you, and one hand for the ship.'

DARREL: 'One hand for you, and one for the ship.'

CASSIDY: Oh lovely, you're getting the hang of it now.

(CASSIDY takes a bottle of beer from his kit bag.)

Next! This ship right, it's a fucking shit ship, alright? It's like a Grimsby ship. Shit.

(He puts the bottle of beer on the table and it rolls to port, stage right.)

It's gorra list.

(He opens the bottle and drinks.)

Here we are in Hull, in dock, a thousand miles from the Arctic and we already gorra fucking list.

(He takes a second bottle from his bag and hands it to DARREL.)

Here, have a go.

(DARREL puts the bottle on the table – it rolls to port.)

That is a list to port. That's port, over there, and that's starboard. That's forrard, and that's aft.

DARREL: *(Pointing.)* Port, starboard, forrard, aft.

(CASSIDY goes towards him and hugs him.)

CASSIDY: Oh my son, my son! Ha, ha! I knew it! You got the salt in yer blood. You gorra be born to this you know. It's the worst fucking job in the world and only those what is born to it, what has gorrit in the blood, can do it. It's a terrible, terrible hard life and no-one should ever ask a man to go through what we have to go through but, you know –

(He burps.)

– someone's gorra do it.

(CASSIDY opens the second bottle and hands it to DARREL.)

DARREL: Are we allowed to drink?

CASSIDY: No! Definitely not! Very dangerous. No spirituous liquor allowed on board.

(CASSIDY drinks. DARREL drinks.)

Or swearing. Merchant Shipping Act of 1894.

(Tenderly.) Look at yer. Yer look a deckie. Put yer collar over yer jacket. Go on son.

DARREL: I'm gonna tek me jacket off.

CASSIDY: No, no. Go on son. Go on. Just give it a go. For me. Yer collar.

(CASSIDY arranges DARREL's collar over his jacket.)

There. Yer look good. That looks good. Here.

(CASSIDY offers DARREL a cigarette.)

DARREL: I don't smoke. Meks me feel sick.

CASSIDY: *(Laughing.)* No, no, no. You gorra smoke. Here. Tek it.

(CASSIDY lights the cigarette and gives it to him. DARREL takes a drag.)

You're a natural, born to it. I'll bet yer mam dint want you to go, but if you've gorrit in the blood, huh, *que sera* fucking *sera*. Whatever will be will fucking be.

DARREL: She cried.

CASSIDY: The women eh?! They say they don't want you to go to sea, they'd rather you gorra job, I dunno, mekking fucking caravans out at Brough. Caravans. Ha! What sort of a man is proud to stand up and say, 'I make caravans for a living.' A puff that's who. A caravan puff. She dunt want yer to go to sea, does she?

DARREL: I said, she cried.

CASSIDY: Ha, ha, ha! Don't believe a fucking word of it son.
They can't get shot of us quick enough. At home, what,
we're under their feet aren't we? Houses – I don't trust
them, never have. I like a floor to move. You know you're
alive then.

DARREL: Which bunk can I have?

CASSIDY: I'll learn yer everything son. Give me a chance
to mek up for, you know. I'm fucking sorry kid. I ant bin
much of a dad have I? I've tried son, I did try. But... I have
to go to the pub you see.

DARREL: (*Indicating a bunk.*) Can I take this one?

CASSIDY: They call us drunks, but who can judge us eh?
No fucking body! Three weeks gutting, gutting, gutting.
Cawld, fucking cawld, eh! There int a word for how cawld
it is. There's one for yer. When yer hands is frozen, when
yer can't fucking feel them no-more, piss on them. It's hot,
fucking boiling water, brings the blood back. Yeah, you're
gonna enjoy this trip. Piss on yer hands. Write it down, that
one. We're gonna do this proper. Yer gorra pen?

DARREL: Somewhere. I'm sure you're bleeding.

CASSIDY: Another thing! I aren't gonna call yer Snacker.

DARREL: What's a Snacker?

CASSIDY: Deckie Learner. Me, I'm gonna call you son, and
you can call me dad.

DARREL: Please don't call me 'son'.

CASSIDY: Fuck 'em! I don't care what they say. Bastards.
They'll call you Snacker, but I'm gonna call you son.
Fucking hell, I've got the right!

DARREL: I don't want you to call me son!

CASSIDY: Oh no. No, no, no. It's blood. It's love. My only son!

(CASSIDY approaches him as if to hug him again. DARREL backs off and holds him at arm's length.)

DARREL: *(Angry.)* Don't touch me! You're not me dad! I've never met you before in my life! I don't know you. I just met you out there, on the dock. You're not my father. You're drunk.

CASSIDY: Oh no, no, no, yes, yes, it's true, yes, I'm drunk but –

DARREL: You're Cassidy. I've heard about you.

CASSIDY I'm really sorry son.

DARREL: Me dad's called Malcolm. He's a carpet fitter.

CASSIDY: A carpet fitter?

DARREL: That's his job, yeah. Malcolm Ascough. He fits carpets.

CASSIDY: What sort of carpets?

DARREL: Fitted carpets.

(CASSIDY sits and laughs at this.)

CASSIDY: I promise, on my mother's life, God bless her soul, I'm your father.

(DARREL turns away and throws his mattress into a bunk, and climbs in.)

DARREL: I've heard about you.

CASSIDY: What do they say?

DARREL: Dunno.

CASSIDY: Headbanger? Headcase? I've heard the talk. Do they say I ride horses into pubs, eh? Yeah, well, I've only done that once or twice, mebbe three times. I like horses.

I coulda bin a horse jockey, but I was too big, and I was fishing – me whole fucking life. What else have you heard?

DARREL: They say, what I've heard is, that for a laugh you stick fireworks up your arse.

CASSIDY: I can't deny it. At sea you've gorra make your own entertainment. Snowy Gordon took a photo last time but Boots wunt print it. Miserable bastards. I've gorra Catherine wheel in me bag as it happens.

(DARREL climbs out of the bunk.)

DARREL: Everyone in Hull knows about you.

CASSIDY: You've got to understand one thing son. Me father died at sea and his father died at sea, and his father afore him. Fishing, distant water.

DARREL: Your father, your grandfather, and your great grandfather?

CASSIDY: All three of them, yeah. But me great, great grandfather...he's still alive.

(They both laugh.)

He's hiding. Ha!

(They laugh.)

I like you.

DARREL: I'm not your son.

CASSIDY: What's the 'carpet fitter' say about me?

DARREL: He ses yer a one man circus.

CASSIDY: Aye, I've gorra few tricks.

DARREL: He ses you live in Rayners.

CASSIDY: I've gorr house, but our lass won't let me in. Rayners banned me once. The horse I was riding took a shit, in the snug bar. Fucking hell. It's not a big snug is

it, Rayners, and the horse was that big un of Northern
Dairies, the brown Galloway with one eye. They banned
me. Not for long. I started going in Criterion dint I, and I
took everyone with me. So Rayner begged me to go back.
He's changed the doors though. You can't get a horse in
there now.

DARREL: Why do they call you Cassidy? Me dad ses it's not
your name.

CASSIDY: Cos I'm wild like Butch Cassidy, but I ant never
killed no-one. You heard of Butch Cassidy?

DARREL: No.

CASSIDY: He was wild but he dint never kill no-one, like me.
He's in the cowboy books. Here.

*(He slings DARREL a cowboy book from a pile propped up on the
bench.)*

You'll need to know me real name. It's Arthur Duggleby.

DARREL: I'm gonna take this bunk. Will that be alright?

CASSIDY: Fuck 'em! My lad can have any bunk he likes. I
coulda been a skipper you know son. Oh aye, I've got the
ability but I'm colour blind aren't I. Can't be a skipper if
yer can't tell red from green y'see. Ship's lights innit. Red
light's port, green light's starboard. Much the same as not
knowing yer arse from yer elbow. But I could've done it.
Oh yeah.

(He points to his arse and then his elbow.)

Elbow. Arse. See. Easy. Ha, ha!

DARREL: *(Quickly.)* I'm not colour blind.

CASSIDY: That dunt mean nowt. Colour blindness yer catch
off the mother. Fishing, yer got from me. Yer here aren't
yer? Ha, ha! Course you are! The rest of me's A1. Had a
full check up last year. Blood, piss, shit. I had to take in

three separate samples of shit. Each one from different whatsanames.

DARREL: Different movements?

CASSIDY: No, different arseholes.

(They both laugh.)

You're alright kid.

DARREL: Me dad ses you've been in prison.

CASSIDY: Aye, I punched some bloke.

DARREL: Who?

CASSIDY: The Archbishop of York.

DARREL: Why?

CASSIDY: He'd had it coming.

(Beat.) I hate that fucking song of his! I'd told him aforehand I dint want it. At a funeral you gerr a choice of songs like a wedding. 'Eternal Father Strong to Save.' Huh. When's he done any fucking saving, eh?

(Singing.) 'For those in Peril on the Sea.'

Crap. I told him I dint wannit. Meks dying at sea sound like summat to be proud of. Fish and fucking chips! That's what my dad died for. The fish half of a fish and chip supper. But no-one dare say that dare they? They have to dress it all up with words, and music.

(Beat.) I went to the hospital after, see the bishop, and apologise. I thought I'd broken his nose, burr it was already broken, cos he used to be a boxer in the army, can you believe it? A boxing bishop. Fucking hell, what next?

DARREL: Did he forgive yer?

CASSIDY: Oh aye. He's a Christian.

(*Beat. Tenderly.*) I got three daughters, all girls. Our lass lost a couple. It turned her that did, but she was badly already. She's gone, her mind's gone. She dunt know who I am. She won't let me in the house. Daren't go out. I buy her a load of tins and leave 'em out the back. I can't wait to get to the fucking Arctic. By time I come back it might have sorted itself out, eh? She might be dead. But that's a bit much to hope for. I dunno son?

DARREL: Tut!

CASSIDY: Alright, alright, I won't call you 'son'. Darrel. Aye, I don't know where your mother got that. It's a lass's name int it?

DARREL: (*Momentarily angry.*) No! It int! (*Beat.*) Where are the others?

CASSIDY: They was in Criterion at dinner time, I saw them in there, yeah. We still got an hour afore the tide.

DARREL: Why are you early then?

CASSIDY: I couldn't stay in Cri. I went for a walk. I come across the ship's runner, Percy, talking to one of the coal teamers. He tawld me our Snacker had gone on the Implacable, and that we had a new Snacker this trip. Darrel Ascough. You. But Percy dunt know worr I know! I begged him son! I fucking begged him, burr he wunt listen to me. He wunt have none of it.

DARREL: None of what?

(*Pause.*)

CASSIDY: He dun't know about the dog.

DARREL: What dog?

CASSIDY: My dog! She's my lucky dog you see. I dint know you was on the trip! I swear, son, I dint know you was signed on! I knew you'd be early. Deckie learner, first trip, keen. Yeah, I've planned this. Having a word. Where were we up to?

DARREL: You what?

CASSIDY: Number four. Knocking out the blocks, or knocking out. Very dangerous. Pete Brough, nice lad, he had a skeg over the side when we was knocking out, warp jacknifed, took his head off, clean, like a dandelion. I saw this oilskin walking towards me, walking, fish in one hand, knife in the other, no head. His head went over the wall. So, remember – duck.

DARREL: Knocking out?

CASSIDY: Knocking out the blocks. Gerrin washed over. If you gerr a big sea and you get washed over – don't panic, keep calm. Can you swim?

DARREL: No.

CASSIDY: Good! Excellent. Cos them what can swim are only prolonging the agony.

DARREL: What do I do then, if I get washed over?

CASSIDY: Hang onto the net cos a good skipper never loses a net.

DARREL: What if I 'ant gorr hold of the net?

CASSIDY: (*Laughs. Beat.*) I've got summat I want you to have.

(*CASSIDY begins to empty his kitbag. It is full of beer, fags and fireworks, and little else.*)

DARREL: You've normally gorra dog with you then?

CASSIDY: Oh aye. Jip. She's very clean. Pisses off the same spot on the starboard side. Only had to show her once. Intelligent, you see. Border collie.

DARREL: I wunt mind a dog. Can I have another beer?

CASSIDY: That's more like it! You're gonna be alright Darrel. They'll like you now I've got you smoking and drinking.

DARREL: I dint say I dint like beer.

CASSIDY: Where do you do yer drinking son?

DARREL: Subway club.

CASSIDY: I'm banned from Subway.

DARREL: Yeah?

CASSIDY: I broke forty glasses. It's a trick.

DARREL: What, a trick that went wrong?

CASSIDY: No that's the trick. You pile them up like a pyramid and bang the top one dead hard and all the rest shatter. That's the night I met yer mam.

DARREL: You know me mam?

CASSIDY: Rita, yeah. She's a lovely woman your mother. (*Beat.*) Does she still work there? She was a beauty you know. She won a contest.

DARREL: Miss British Oil and Cake Mills.

CASSIDY: Nineteen-forty...fuck I dunno. How old are you?

DARREL: Seventeen.

CASSIDY: Nineteen-sixty-five tek off seventeen is – hang on – forty-eight. Yeah, so Miss BOCM nineteen-forty-seven. Bloody hell, time flies.

DARREL: Why forty-seven? And not forty-eight?

CASSIDY: She had to carry you for nine month dint she.

DARREL: What? You –

CASSIDY: I couldn't make it work. It was her fault, she'd let the contest go to her head. She ran off with some flash bastard from Scarborough with an Arial Square Four.

(A ship's horn sounds twice, a tenor. A second ship's horn replies, a bass.)

Where's yer dad from?

(Pause. Beat.) Did he have an Arial Square Four?

DARREL: I dunno.

CASSIDY: *(Tenderly.)* Does he look like you? Do you look like him?

(Pause.)

DARREL: No. Not at all.

CASSIDY: I look a bit like you. You look a bit like me. You're just a strip of a lad but –

DARREL: – Why are you telling me this? You're telling me you're my father. You're telling me me dad is not me dad, that me mother…that you're me real dad. Why? I mean, what I mean is…why now?

CASSIDY They'll be here soon, and once we're off, we'll get no privacy. I got summat for yer. I don't want them to see. This might be me last trip.

DARREL: What?

CASSIDY: Oh yeah. Old Father Neptune's been nipping at my arse for fucking years, and one of these days…well, yeah, you never know. And I've alles relied on me dog for luck.

DARREL: You're terrible drunk aren't yer?

CASSIDY: Hope I am. I spent enough money on it.

(From out of the kitbag CASSIDY has found a small package, like a large purse, made out of rubber.)

Here we are. I want you to have this.

DARREL: What is it?

CASSIDY: A duck suit. Navy issue survival suit. You wear it – look – if you're going down, and you know you're going down, so you have to gerr in a raft or go over the wall, then get in some dry long johns and socks and that and then put this on over the top. Water tight, air tight. You don't swim do yer? Well, mebbe if you fart a couple of times it'll keep you afloat, who knows. It's yours.

DARREL: Have you got one?

CASSIDY: That's mine.

(*Beat.*) Now there's another thing. There's summat I want you to have. A betting slip, it's worth three hundred quid. Yeah! I live on North Hull estate, d'yer know it?

DARREL: Yeah.

CASSIDY: Twennie-first ave, number eleven, legs eleven, you won't forget. The betting slip's in a tin of creosote out in the scullery. Our lass won't let you in but go to the Bethel, take the priest with yer, she'll open the door to him, then just say that I'd said if owt ever happened to me I'd said you're to have the creosote. Alright? But don't open the tin indoors, tek the whole tin and fuck off.

DARREL: Don't open the tin in there?

CASSIDY: No! I don't trust that priest.

(*Noises off. The other lads are arriving. DARREL stands and faces the door and listens. CASSIDY stands.*)

The lads are here.

DECKIE 1: (*Off.*) Eh Ray! D'yer hear about Cassidy!?

RAY: (*Off.*) Yer late get yer arses below!

DECKIE 2: (*Off.*) He's killed the dog!

RAY: (*Off and a shouted whisper.*) Fuck! The mad bastard.

DECKIE 1: (*Off.*) He slit her throat in Criterion, in the lounge. Blood everyfuckingwhere.

RAY: (*Off.*) Jesus Christ!

DECKIE 2: (*Off.*) They've banned him again.

DECKIE 1: (*Off.*) He took his gutting knife, held her by the ears, and just ran it across her throat, stood up and walked out.

(Silence. Broken by a ship's horn, a tenor. The second horn, a bass, replies.)

DARREL: You killed the dog?

CASSIDY: Aye.

DARREL: In the pub?

CASSIDY: Aye.

DARREL: And you're me dad? Me father?

CASSIDY: Aye. Sorry.

(To black.)

The James Joyce

Blackout.

The sound of the James Joyce head to wind and dodging in a Force Nine. The engine is at half speed. At roughly two minute intervals a big water breaks over the whaleback. There is the sound of two men on the whaleback chopping ice from the deck and upperworks. Before each big wave there is heard a scream of 'WATER!!' The chopping stops on this shout, the wave breaks twenty seconds later, and then the chopping resumes. This cycle is heard twice.

Lights up.

It is 1972. The forecastle of the James Joyce. There are clothes, socks, and underpants drying all over the place. Books, and pornography on the table. A large colour centrefold of a naked model on a bed in high heels has replaced the 1965 black and white model. NORMAN's bunk is downstage right. It is wallpapered with pornography. Directly above him is ROC's bunk with no pin ups, but a large pile of cowboy books. Upstage right on the bottom tier is BILL's bunk which is neat and tidy. On the stage left side of the forecastle is BAGNALL's bunk which is on the bottom tier upstage. The Snacker's bunk is downstage left on the bottom tier. DARREL's bunk is downstage on the top tier. DARREL has some novels and a picture of his wife and family. BILL is sitting at the table carving and painting the jawbone of a cod to form a decorative butterfly. Others, already completed, are put to one side. He has a rollie tab stuck to the corner of his lip. ROC is lying in his bunk staring at the ceiling. DARREL is sat at the table smoking. NORMAN is pacing about. BAGNALL and the Snacker are off. They're all in vests, singlets, long johns, underpants. NORMAN has a David Bowie T-shirt and blue and white Y-fronts over a pair of tan woman's tights.

NORMAN: Daz?

DARREL: What?

NORMAN: Fag.

DARREL: Tut!

(DARREL lights a cigarette for him and passes it over. NORMAN takes a drag. He slams his fist against the bulwark, then headbutts it.)

DARREL: Whatsamatter Norm?

NORMAN: Nothing.

BILL: Ha, ha, ha, ha!

NORMAN: What makes you think there's owt up wi me?

DARREL: Dunno.

NORMAN: I wanna cup of cocoa!

(NORMAN fists the bulwark a second time and then a third.)

I want some fucking cocoa! Or tea. Pot of shackles. Anything! Eh!?

BILL: Shutup and sit yer arse down. Ha, ha, ha.

NORMAN: Let's draw lots for gonna get some tea. Big pot of tea, and cocoa for me. Eh! We'll draw lots.

DARREL: Sit down Norman. Canasta?

(DARREL starts dealing from a double Canasta pack.)

NORMAN: No! I want cocoa.

DARREL: *(To BILL.)* You in Bill?

BILL: No. I'm happy. Ha, ha, ha, ha.

NORMAN: And summat to fucking eat. When did we last eat? Fuck!

DARREL: Roc! You in?

ROC: No ta.

NORMAN: We'll draw lots, eh? What d'yer say?

(ROC pulls himself up on one elbow and watches NORMAN and DARREL.)

DARREL: So if you lose the draw, what you gonna do?

NORMAN: The loser er...fuck... I dunno. The loser gets all their gear on, and goes up and across the foredeck, to the galley, get the cook to brew up.

DARREL: That's my point. You, Norman. You lose, you get yer gear on, run across the foredeck, to the galley, get a pot of tea, some shackles –

NORMAN: Cocoa –

DARREL: Cocoa for yourself, and what...run back across the deck – hanging on with what, eh? How yer gonna hang on? Wrap yer knob round summat like a monkey.

BILL: Ha, ha, ha! Yeah, Norm, hang on with yer knob.

NORMAN: Shutup yer daft old git.

BILL: Monkey knob! Ha, ha, ha, ha. (*BILL makes monkey noises.*)

DARREL: You'd do that? If you lost?

NORMAN: Yeah.

DARREL: Next Sheffield flood you would. I've been four years with you in this ship Norman and I can tell you that you would not do that.

NORMAN: Are you calling me a liar?

DARREL: Yeah. You're banking on someone else losing.

NORMAN: You're a fucking clever git you. What school was it again?

DARREL: Archbishop William Temple.

NORMAN: Yeah, exactly. Fucking nuns.

(*To ROC.*) What're you looking at you big daft beswick?

ROC: You.

DARREL: You're starting to get on my tits Norman.

NORMAN: Tits? I wunt be surprised. You gorra lass's name.

DARREL: (*Angry.*) Fuck off. Wanker.

BILL: I like an happy crew. Ha, ha, ha, ha.

DARREL: (*To BILL.*) It's not on Bill, having the Snacker on the whaleback. Fuck, he's only a kid.

BILL: Na, he'll be alright.

DARREL: No-one ever asked me to crack ice when I was a Snacker. Not in owt as bad as this.

ROC: Bagnall will keep an eye out for him.

BILL: Ha, ha, I bet Baggy wishes he'd gone to that wedding in Fleetwood now, ha, ha, ha!

DARREL: Working with a line on is a bloody art, you know it is. Summat you gorra learn.

BILL: He'll be learning then won't he. Ha, ha!

ROC: He's got Baggy with him.

DARREL: Bagnall?! That Lancastrian bastard's only interested in number one.

NORMAN: Tut! Three days stuck down here, with you lot. Rabbit, rabbit, rabbit. No cocoa. Fucking twat's lark this is. I mean, where we going?!

ROC: We're dodging.

NORMAN: Dodging! Going bloody nowhere! We're standing still!

BILL: Aye, many a time I've seen it as bad as this, and there int nowt you can do but head to wind and –

NORMAN: Shut it will yer! Why can't we go in?!

DARREL: Sit down Norman will yer.

NORMAN: Find a fucking fjord!

DARREL: Yer know why.

NORMAN: I know fucking nothing. Not bin paid to bloody think am I. My last trip this.

DARREL: What yer gonna do then Norm?

ROC: He's gonna be a bus driver.

(BILL and DARREL laugh.)

NORMAN: (*To ROC.*) Shut it!

DARREL: You can't even drive a car Norman. He can't drive can he Roc?

ROC: Na. Course he can't.

NORMAN: Driving a bus is easier int it?

DARREL: How come?

NORMAN: Yer gerr a set route.

(All but NORMAN laugh. BILL stops what he is doing and laughs irritatingly longer.)

BILL: Ha, ha, ha, ha, ha, ha.

(Beat.) Ha, ha, ha, ha, ha.

(Beat.) You gerr a set route. Ha, ha, ha, ha, ha, ha, ha.

(A big wave hits and silences them all.)

DARREL: (*To BILL.*) You'll have to use the buses when they move you out of Flinton Street.

NORMAN: Yeah, well there'll be no laughing on my bus.

(*To BILL.*) You're not moving nowhere near me I hope?

BILL: Bransholme.

NORMAN: Fuck. That's just over the back. If I can hear that laughing of yours I'm ringing the police.

BILL: Ha, ha! They're giving us a garden. Might gerr a shed. Na! Our lass likes to see what I'm up to.

DARREL: Gerra greenhouse then.

BILL: Aye, that's a possibility. Ha, ha.

NORMAN: What's wrong with the house you got?

BILL: It's onny a sham four. Two bedrooms for nine of us.

NORMAN: You're never there.

BILL: Corporation don't like it. Outside loo. No bathroom. They're gonna knock it down.

DARREL: It's insanitary.

BILL: It is insane, yeah. It's bloody madness. Perfectly good house.

NORMAN: (*To BILL.*) Kaw! I won't be fishing when I'm your age.

BILL: I've got seven daughters. Do you know how much tiaras cost?

ROC: How's your mortgage work Daz?

DARREL: You're just buying your house on tick that's all. Takes twennie-five years, and then it's yours.

BILL: In debt for twennie-five years. That's not manly.

NORMAN: What?! Gerr on with yer butterflies yer fucking headbanger. How did I get stuck with you lot? I coulda signed on the Faraday you know. You know where they've gone don't yer. Godshaven. Oh yeah.

DARREL: (*Sarcastic.*) Ooh Godshaven.

NORMAN: Yeah, Eskimo birds everywhere. Gagging for it.

DARREL: You believe all that do you?

NORMAN: It's a known fact. You see, it's illegal to be pregnant in Greenland.

DARREL: Bollocks.

NORMAN: Tis! Run by Denmark innit nowadays. If they get up the duff they fly them off to Denmark which is what they all want any road, and they spend the rest of their lives on the dole mekking slippers.

BILL: Aye, they do mek smashing slippers. Fur slippers. I've bought a couple of pairs for our lass over the years.

NORMAN: You dock in Godshaven and they surround the ship, begging for it. Twennie, thirty, forty Eskimo birds. All up for it.

ROC: Where are all their men?

NORMAN: The fuck do I know? Skiing.

DARREL: You've been to Godshaven Bill.

(NORMAN sits and picks up his cards, and begins to sort them.)

BILL: Many a time.

DARREL: Tell him it's not true.

NORMAN: Course it's true.

BILL: I always got a shag out of it.

NORMAN: (*To DARREL.*) Told yer!

(*To ROC.*) Are you listening?

(*To BILL.*) Bet your lass dunt know eh? Ha! She thought you was off fishing but there you are shagging your way round the arctic circle. No wonder she gets plenty of slippers.

BILL: Aye, I went in there once on the Kingston Jet when we'd snagged the prop. Five days we was in there. Ha, ha, ha. We had Cassidy with us –

NORMAN: Oh fuck, Cassidy! I shoulda known.

BILL: Cass gorrit all organised. We had a donkey hose rigged
up in the fishroom and the galley boy's job was to hose 'em
down, cos they used to stink you know cos they eat nowt
but meat and fish, you wunt wanna kiss 'em.

NORMAN: They'd be disappointed then! Ha!

(All laugh.)

BILL: And then Cassidy'd sent 'em in here for the business.

NORMAN: What – an orgy?

BILL: No, no, no. It weren't an orgy. Ha, ha! It were like a
big sort of endless piss up where everybody's on the job all
over the shop.

NORMAN: That's an orgy! That is the word for that sort of a
sex party come piss up.

BILL: Na, there wan't nowt Roman about it.

NORMAN: Who said the fucking Romans have to be invited?
Daz? Look it up in that dictionary of yours will yer.

DARREL: 'Orgy'.

(DARREL goes to get his dictionary.)

BILL: Na, it wasn't an orgy. Just a big party with a lot of
booze, and Cassidy playing the piana, and everyone
fucking the eskimo birds.

NORMAN: That's an orgy!

ROC: How come you had a piana?

BILL: Cass was in Rayners the night before the tide and they
was chucking out the old one. So Cass put it on a cart and
took it down the ship, and we had on the portside of the
foredeck all trip.

NORMAN: You expect me to believe that you daft old cunt.

BILL: I don't care what you think.

DARREL: (*Reading from a Penguin Paperback dictionary.*) Orgy. 'A wild gathering marked by promiscuous sexual activity.'

NORMAN: See, that was an orgy!

BILL: I was there! It wan't an orgy. There was a lot of shagging and drinking but…

NORMAN: – Shutup will yer! You see?!

BILL: Aye, I sailed with Cassidy a few times. Always had that lucky dog with him. Ha, ha, ha! All the arctic circle to shit in and where does she go? On my winch handle. Ha, ha, ha.

NORMAN: Happy days. Sharing a ship with the laughing policeman.

BILL: Aye, we won't see the likes of Cassidy again. One time I was with him on the Lord –

NORMAN: (*In BILL's face.*) – Shut it! Alright! No more fucking Cassidy stories.

ROC: Norman!

NORMAN: What!? I'm sick of him. It's like living with the seven dwarves.

(*A big wave hits with a bang. It throws them into a momentary list. They stop talking, and wait for the ship to right itself. SILENCE. The ship comes back.*)

Let's talk about…I dunno…horses. Race horses. If I win the pools I wunt mind a racehorse.

(*Pause.*)

Horses.

BILL: Cassidy wanted to be a jockey you know.

(NORMAN turns and starts to head for BILL but ROC sticks a hand out of his bunk and holds him back by the collar.)

NORMAN: Gerroff! I'll brae hell out of him.

(NORMAN goes over to the stage left bulwark and presses his head against it.)

BILL: You wanna get yersen a nice little lass and get married. And stop paying for it, and stop talking about it, stop thinking about it and gerr on and do it proper for a change.

ROC: Leave it Bill, yeah? The two of yer.

BILL: Forget the pools. I could save you a load of money.

NORMAN: Oh yeah, what would you do?

BILL: Cut yer chopper off.

NORMAN: I'll do what I fucking like. It's my knob.

BILL: Monkey knob. Ha, ha, ha, ha.

NORMAN: I'll have you.

BILL: Get yersen a nice little lass. Settle down. Like Daz here.

DARREL: Yeah, a family Norman.

BILL: Family. That's all there is.

NORMAN: Tut!

BILL: I'd had three daughters by the time I was your age. You, huh, you're still living with your mother, buying them magazines from Lollipop.

NORMAN: I'll shut your mouth for you soon grandad.

BILL: You should tell him Roc, you're his mate.

NORMAN: He ant gorr owt to say on the subject.

BILL: *(To Roc.)* You still going out with that Maureen from up National Ave?

ROC: Yeah.

BILL: She'd be good for you Roc. Mek a good wife. Aye, looks aren't everything you know.

NORMAN: That int nowt.

ROC: Yes, it is.

NORMAN: No it int!

ROC: What am I doing then?

NORMAN: You're not like going out with her are yer. You just know her.

BILL: Maureen. It's a lovely name.

ROC: Yeah.

NORMAN: (*To DARREL.*) What you reading?

DARREL: Fuck off.

BILL: (*To NORMAN.*) I've never had to pay for it you know, me whole life I've…

NORMAN: Shurrup Cassanova.

ROC: I'm gonna ask her to marry me. When I get back this time.

BILL: Oh smashing.

NORMAN: You what?

ROC: I'm gonna marry Maureen.

NORMAN: No you aren't! You don't love her! Tell him Daz, he dunt wanna be going around gerrin hissen wed to women he dunt love.

DARREL: Do you love her Roc?

ROC: I dunno. How do you tell?

34

NORMAN: How do you tell? You don't have to think...
when...for Christ's sake! You don't love her! And that's
that.

ROC: How do you know?

NORMAN: You don't know the first thing about owt when it
comes to women.

ROC: I'm gonna ask her to marry me. When I get back. Have
a family.

DARREL: Good on yer Roc. You do what you want. Don't
listen to Norman.

NORMAN: Shutup you. Who's side are you on? He doesn't
fucking love her! Stop encouraging him will yer. Fuck. I'm
the one who's got to live with the consequences.

DARREL: What's it got to do with you?

NORMAN: Tut! You...you don't understand. It's just this shit
we're in. It's turned his mind.

(*To Roc.*) Med you all thoughtful.

BILL: Do you really love her Roc?

NORMAN: For Christ's sake!

ROC: I dunno. I think I might do. Like I say, I'm not sure.

BILL: Would yer use her shit as toothpaste?

NORMAN: You what?

DARREL: Would you use her shit as toothpaste?

(*ROC is thinking and all of them look to him for an answer. ROC
takes the question seriously.*)

ROC: No. No, I wouldn't.

BILL: You don't love her then.

NORMAN: (*To BILL.*) That's the first sensible thing you've said for three days, now shut it, and get on with yer butterflies. How many of them bloody things are yer gonna do?

BILL: Seven, eight. Eight. One for each of me daughters and one for our lass.

NORMAN: Seven daughters. And no sons. You must be doing summat wrong.

ROC: I'm still gonna ask her. I'm gonna get wed.

DARREL: She might say no Roc.

NORMAN: You're kidding aren't yer. Who the fuck else is gonna marry her?

(NORMAN pulls a grotesque face.)

BILL: What heats a room? The fire or the mantlepiece? Knowhatimean?

(Pause. They're confused.)

NORMAN: He's on gas.

ROC: Yeah. North Sea Gas.

NORMAN: (*To BILL.*) He's on gas.

BILL: (*To NORMAN.*) Least he's gorra woman. That's your lass there. A picture. You can't fuck her, she can't mek a pot of tea, and she an't even got the manners to tek her shoes off afore she gets into bed. If she was here, on this table, now, then she'd be worth tekking note of. I'd gerr interested. But a picture. Ha, ha, ha, ha, ha.

NORMAN: Oh aye, she'd jump on a stinkie old shellback like you, yeah?

BILL: I could give her a good time which is more –

NORMAN: I know about women!

(*To DARREL.*) Fag.

DARREL: That's twennie-seven you owe me now.

(*DARREL lights a fag for him and passes it over.*)

BILL: You don't learn owt about women, or what they want, when you're paying for it.

NORMAN: I know enough. The love button.

(*DARREL and BILL laugh.*)

What? That's all you need to know. Find that little bald headed bastard and yer laughing.

(*DARREL and BILL laugh again.*)

DARREL: What I like most about being married, and back me up on this one Bill, if you agree, is, you know, just lying in on a morning, say you've had a good trip, settled up, everything's alright, you've given her a good night out in a club or summat, and then in the morning, she's got the kids off to school and then she comes back to bed, you know, and you're all cuddled up like, and yer just loop yer arm round and cup a tit, just hold it, and then yer drift off to sleep again.

BILL: Smashing.

DARREL: Lovely.

(*NORMAN gets into his bunk which is down stage right on the lower tier. He starts to read a pornographic magazine but throws it to one side as a big wave hits. He grips the side of his bunk in fear. The ship rights herself.*)

I'm not saying the sex int important it's just that –

NORMAN: Fuck! I'll be glad when I'm back on that whaleback cracking ice.

(*To ROC.*) When's our watch?

ROC: Half-hour yet.

BILL: Get yer head down. Get some sleep.

NORMAN: Huh.

BILL: Who's gonna be yer best man Roc?

NORMAN: He's not gerrin' married.

BILL: Norman int it. Stands to reason. Yer best mate's always best man.

NORMAN: I aren't backing you up marrying someone you don't love. What kind of a mate is that?

ROC: I haven't asked you yet.

NORMAN: Who else is there? Bloody hell I've been wiping your arse since you was a kid. I mean, I've fucking earned the right ant I?

DARREL: You said you wunt do it!

NORMAN: I mean, earned the right to be asked. I gorra few jokes.

ROC: I don't want any mucky jokes at my wedding. Her mother dunt like deckies as it is.

NORMAN: Fuck her mother.

BILL: Where you gonna have reception? In, you know, in like an ideal world.

ROC: Subway club.

NORMAN: Subway? In an ideal world you'd like to have your wedding reception in Subway club? D'yer hear that Daz?

DARREL: Yeah.

(NORMAN gets out of his bunk.)

NORMAN: In an ideal world, you know, money no object, Frank Rocco chooses Subway. Tut! This is the sort of shit I have to put up with.

ROC: I like Subway.

NORMAN: No, no, no! You're not fucking listening. Bill said in an 'ideal world' – like dream world – win the fucking pools world.

ROC: I don't do the pools.

NORMAN: (*Sighs.*) Oh fuck. Get more sense out of a fucking shovel.

BILL: I'll sing at the wedding if yer like.

(*Singing.*) Ave Maria. Ave Maria. Ave Maria.

I've gorr an LP with fifteen different versions of Ave Maria on it.

ROC: What's the LP called?

BILL: Ave Maria.

(A big bang as a big wave hits. It throws the James Joyce into a momentary list to starboard. The engines are heard to scream on full ahead as the skipper drives it out of the list and back to dodging. A list to starboard remains. The crew in the forecastle are aware of it. Silence.)

ROC: Does your mam still work in Subway Daz?

DARREL: Lunch times, yeah.

ROC: Do you think that'd be possible? A wedding reception.

DARREL: Are you a member?

ROC: No.

BILL: You can do better than Subway Roc. I've been to receptions in there. They hardly put themselves out do they? Stick a bit of plywood over the snooker tables, and pay the stripper to keep her clothes on. Ha, ha, ha.

NORMAN: I'm not standing up in Subway and mekking a fool of mesen.

DARREL: No-one's asked you to.

NORMAN: Oh come on! Who else has he got?

BILL: Are you a member Norm?

NORMAN: Subway? Fuck off.

ROC: He joined three clubs after the last trip. Andrews, Nash, and Stevedores and Dockers.

DARREL: *(With contempt.)* Dockers?

NORMAN: *(Getting out of his bunk.)* I was drunk!

DARREL: You dint pay full annual memberships?

NORMAN: I was pissed!

DARREL: You're at sea forty weeks of the year.

NORMAN: He shoulda bin looking after me, but he ant got the brains he was born with. I only joined so I can bona fide him in or we'd both be standing in the street all Saturday night.

BILL: But you dint join Subway?

NORMAN: I can't stand Subway!

(BILL and DARREL laugh.)

ROC: It's alright Subway.

NORMAN: Why dint you join it then?

ROC: I don't see the point of paying out for annual membership when I'm at sea forty weeks of the year.

(BILL and DARREL laugh.)

NORMAN: You coulda joined to bona fide me in for a change.

ROC: You don't like Subway.

(BILL and DARREL laugh.)

NORMAN: Alright, alright! Come on gerron with yer butterflies. How many have you done now?

BILL: Five.

NORMAN: We'll be running out of fish soon. What is that?

BILL: Yeah, Red Admiral.

NORMAN: Who's that for?

BILL: My little lass. Lizzie. The youngest.

NORMAN: How old's she then?

BILL: Thirty-two.

NORMAN: It's a fucking zoo this.

(He stands and paces again.)

Where are we?!

DARREL: Same place we were yesterday, and the day before, and the day before that.

BILL: Aye, you don't go no place when you're dodging.

NORMAN: Why don't we go in? East coast of Iceland. That's near enough int it?

DARREL: We're off the West Coast.

NORMAN: East, West – what's the difference?

DARREL: You know why we don't go in.

NORMAN: We're dodging. I'm not the old man, I'm not saying I am, but why can't we just sort of edge towards the coast.

DARREL: Stop dodging you mean?

NORMAN: I don't mean…oh fuck…I dunno. What're you reading? Cowboys?

DARREL: A novel.

NORMAN: You're a clever arsed bastard aren't yer? Are you gonna go for yer skipper's ticket?

DARREL: Yeah. Got me medical when we get back.

BILL: Cassidy was the best seaman I've ever met but he was colour blind, couldn't be a skipper.

NORMAN: Shut the fuck up! If I hear one more thing about Cassidy I'll fucking do you.

(*To DARREL.*) Yeah, I can see you hiding away up in that glass sowester. Not much point staying in this game if yer can't work your way up.

(*NORMAN snatches a paperback novel from DARREL's grasp. He looks with contempt at the arty cover.*)

Let's have a look at this crap then.

(*He flicks the book open and starts to read to himself.*)

Ha! Fucking hell! *A Portrait of the Artist as a Young Man.* James Joyce. Oi! James Joyce! 'Once upon a time...' Yeah! Once upon a fucking time. Do they all live happily ever after?

DARREL: I an't finished it, 'ave I...

NORMAN: (*Tossing the book back to DARREL.*) Shite!

(*Beat.*) How long can it keep this up?

BILL: I've seen worse than this. I was in Isafjiord that night in sixty-eight.

DARREL: (*Sharply.*) Alright, Bill. We don't need that.

BILL: The wind was coming off that hill at hundred, hundred and ten, and the air was cawlder than the sea, cos it's not an hill it's a glacier –

NORMAN: (*Desperate, to DARREL.*) Are you gonna stop him?

DARREL: Sit down Norman.

BILL: Forty ships, all iced up like Christmas trees. Then the Ross Cleveland started heeling over. She was only half a cable off to port. But there was nowt you could do. Ah, but that wind was a hundred and ten. This is nowt.

NORMAN: I could put up with this shit if I had some cocoa, knoworrimean?

ROC: Yeah.

NORMAN: (*To BILL.*) You finished?

BILL: He knows what he's doing does the old man. Yer just gorra sit it out.

NORMAN: Yeah, well I've been sitting it out for three days now and me arse has gone on strike. I want summat to eat, and summat to drink.

(*To DARREL.*) This wunt have happened if your lass hadn't waved.

DARREL: Crap.

NORMAN: It's unlucky. Women – waving at ships.

DARREL: (*Miming.*) It's a medical condition she's got. Goodbye elbow.

NORMAN: I wun't let any wife of mine come down dock and wave.

DARREL: You don't have a wife.

NORMAN: If! They'll be alright on that submarine won't they? They'll just go under this. Tut! They have women on board you know, the Ruskies. Big Russian birds with hairy tits. They catch summat off the engines.

BILL: Radiation.

NORMAN: That's it. If you're a bloke it'll give you a pair of tits. A hairy pair. Had to go into Murmansk once for the hospital. Kaw! Prossies everywhere. I speak a bit of

43

Russian you know. Yo cocho fuck. I'd like a fuck. Ostar Oshno Ya epileptic. Take care I'm epileptic.

BILL: Cassidy was based in Murmansk during the war. Running ball bearings on them motor gun boats.

NORMAN: (*To DARREL.*) You know what I mean!

BILL: He got the Conspicuous Gallantry medal for that. Victoria Cross, as good as, that is. Ha, ha.

NORMAN: (*Shouting at BILL.*) It's 1972! Chicory Tip are number one! Inside his head Cassidy's still fighting the second world war!

BILL: Aye, you won't see his like again. Best skipper I ever sailed with was –

NORMAN: – oh God!

BILL: – Phil Waudby. He could find fish in a fucking farmyard! Ha, ha! Yeah, fascinating Phil we used to call him, ha, ha, ha.

ROC: What d'yer call him that for?

BILL: Cos he was a really interesting man. Aye, they're all gone, them, proper trawlermen. You sailed with Cassidy dint yer Darrel, when the Kingston Jet went down?

DARREL: What about it?

ROC: They say Cass went back for the dog.

NORMAN: Oh don't encourage them.

DARREL: I was in the other raft.

BILL: Na, not the dog, it was Eggy Barrat's wedding ring.

NORMAN: That's what I heard. Is that true?

DARREL: I said. I was in the other raft. It was night.

(*Big wave hits. The ship comes back. A period of silence.*)

BILL: They all got out and got in two rafts when Eggy Barratt
pipes up, 'I've left me wedding ring in me bunk, our lass'll
kill me' – so Cass dives in and swims back to the ship,
climbs on board, a sinking ship remember, and he waves
at everyone like the daft bastard he was and goes down
into the forecastle, comes back up on top, chucks the ring
to the raft, goes back down under the whaleback, and then
she slips under.

ROC: That right Daz?

DARREL: (*Pedantically.*) I was in the other fucking raft!

BILL: They never found his body. I wunt be surprised if he
don't walk in Rayners one night, or ride in on a bloody
hoss of course. Lived by different rules did Cassidy, so
mebbe he's gorr his own rules in death. Aye, I knew
Cassidy, they brock the mould there. Ha, ha, ha, ha, ha. A
one man circus.

DARREL: Come on then! Let's draw lots. I'm fucking
starving. Eh?

NORMAN: Yeah.

DARREL: Bill?

BILL: What?

DARREL: Someone go and get a pot of shackles. Draw lots.

BILL: That cook can't mek shackles.

NORMAN: (*To DARREL.*) Just deal the cards!

(*DARREL deals four cards.*)

Aces high. Lowest card loses.

(*They take their cards.*)

BILL: Ace.

NORMAN: Jammy. King.

ROC: Three.

DARREL: Five.

NORMAN: Fuck!

(NORMAN fists the bulwark.)

Best of three? Don't go Roc.

ROC: I lost.

NORMAN: Fuck that! Oh shit Roc, come on!

ROC: I'm gonna get your fucking cocoa now shurrup.

(NORMAN grabs hold of ROC's shirt.)

NORMAN: No Roc, no, no! You don't understand! Just forget it Roc, eh!

ROC: I lost.

DARREL: I'll go. I don't mind going.

(DARREL goes to his locker and gets his kit bag out. During the next he takes out his duck suit, changes into clean dry gear and puts the duck suit on. NORMAN continues to hang onto ROC's shirt.)

BILL: Eh, come on, let's just forget the whole idea, eh?

DARREL: There's a lifeline to the winches. I've bin listening. There's a big sea every two minutes or so. Just a matter of timing int it.

BILL: *(To DARREL.)* What the fuck's that?

DARREL: A duck suit.

BILL: Where'dyer gerrit?

DARREL: Me dad give it me.

BILL: He's a carpet fitter in't he? Does he do a lot of damp basements then?! Ha, ha, ha.

NORMAN: Shutup you fucking half wit!

ROC: Was he navy?

DARREL: Reserves.

(A big sea hits. NORMAN grabs a hold of his bunk in fear.)

NORMAN: Oh God!

ROC: Alright Norm. The old man knows worr he's doing.

BILL: These is the best sea ships there is these you know. It's them big stern trawlers that can't tek a sea. We just go up and down like a cork.

(ROC puts a hand out on NORMAN's shoulder. He is shaking.)

NORMAN: *(To ROC.)* Gerroff. I'm alright.

DARREL: Quiet!

BILL: What is it son?

DARREL: Wait!

NORMAN: What?!

DARREL: They've not gone back on top.

ROC: You what?

DARREL: They're not chopping no more.

BILL: Wa, they'll have the donkey hose on by now.

DARREL: You'd still be chopping. One with the hose and one chopping.

NORMAN: What are you gerrin at?!

ROC: Calm down Norman.

(ROC puts out a hand to NORMAN, but NORMAN pushes it away.)

NORMAN: Gerroff. What do yer mean?!

ROC: Norm. It's alright.

DARREL: Bagnall and Snacker have been on the whaleback past couple of hours cracking ice, same as we were, and now, they've stopped.

(Silence. They listen. There is no chopping, no banging.)

BILL: Dunt mean nowt.

DARREL: No, it dunt mean nowt. I'm not saying it does. The old man's probably got them working on the upperworks, or the wheelhouse, or some place else.

NORMAN: That's not what you're saying!

ROC: Shutup Norman!

DARREL: *(To Roc.)* Get him calmed down will yer!

BILL: This int nowt much.

(DARREL goes out to the drying room and returns with his boots, sou'wester, and oil frock. He puts them on.)

DARREL: *(To NORMAN.)* I'll get you some cocoa Norm. It'll be alright. Sugar, yeah?

NORMAN: Yeah. Two.

DARREL: Alright.

(DARREL exits up the companionway.)

ROC: I shoulda gone.

NORMAN: No!

ROC: I could mek a ship to shore. Talk to Maureen. Propose.

NORMAN: You don't wanna marry her you big fucking stupid lump! Whatsamarrer with yer? Look...she's a tart.

BILL: Oooh! Now then, ha, ha, ha!

NORMAN: *(To BILL.)* Shut it! This is private!

ROC: It's not fair on Maureen that. She's quiet. She's not really been with anyone. She dun't dye her hair.

NORMAN: She's a filthy, filthy, fucking slag! She's trying to get you Roc, can't you see that. Whatsamarrer with yer?

ROC: Stop saying whatsamarrer with me. There int nowt wrong with me.

NORMAN: She's trying to trap you, she's gonna...

ROC: What? What is she gonna do? I can see what she's trying to do and mebbe that's what I want!

NORMAN: She's a slag, she's...

ROC: I know what you did. She told me. We talk.

NORMAN: What did she tell you?

(Beat.) She fucked me! I wasn't interested!

BILL: Oh bloody hell.

NORMAN: She forced me, you godda believe me. I wan't gonna touch her!

ROC: It's nice to have someone you can talk with.

(BAGNALL enters down the companionway. He is the third hand and has an air of authority. He is wearing full sea gear, sou'wester, oil frock, gloves, sea boots. He goes straight in the drying room and takes his gear off. ROC lights a cigarette for him and takes it in.)

(Off.) Here you go Baggy.

BAGNALL: *(Off.)* Ta.

(ROC comes back in.)

NORMAN: Snacker?! Snacker?! Where's the kid?!

ROC: Don't say nothing.

(BAGNALL enters. He's down to his long johns. He is carrying a bottle of rum.)

Is he gonna go in?

BAGNALL: In where?

ROC: Dunno. Isafjiord.

BAGNALL: We're blind now. We've lost the scanner.

NORMAN: Ohhh!

BAGNALL: What's the matter with him?

ROC: He's alright.

BAGNALL: Block of ice came off the upperworks.

NORMAN: (*Quiet but intense.*) Oh fuck!

(*NORMAN begins to rock.*)

BILL: What you doing down here Baggy? You gorr another bell yet?

BAGNALL: The old man has sent me down with this here bottle of rum.

(*ROC starts gathering the tot glasses and takes the bottle from BAGNALL.*)

BILL: We've had our rum, this watch.

BAGNALL: Don't want none then? The old man ain't having no-one on't whaleback. He ses he wouldn't wanna be doing that himself, quite rightly, and so he ain't got the heart to tell no-one else to do it. Any road, you can only work for so long, and then you gorra get yourself out of the way. There's a greener every couple of minutes. We weren't doing no good as it happens.

(*ROC distributes the tot glasses. They drink.*)

BILL: Sweethearts and wives. May they never meet. Ha, ha.

(*No-one laughs. It's an old joke.*)

BAGNALL: He's got Spud and Jimmy working the donkey hose on the boat deck. Trying to clear the rafts. They're about three foot under with ice.

ROC: Where's Snacker?

(Pause.)

BAGNALL: He went over the wall.

NORMAN: (*Quietly.*) Ohhhhhh!

ROC: He got washed over?

BAGNALL: Aye. It were a big un. I thought you'd have heard it.

ROC: We did.

NORMAN: Ohhhhh! I need a shit.

ROC: Go on then. Tek a shit.

(NORMAN maintains a constant low moan.)

BAGNALL: The old man ses if any of yer wanna go up there, the wheelhouse that is, he'll let you do ship to shore. I've rung Fleetwood.

BILL: Have you now?

BAGNALL: Aye, rang me father. Couple of bits of business.

ROC: Can you get to the wheelhouse?

BAGNALL: I wouldn't bother trying, like I say, unless you've got some business.

BILL: Is Daz alright?

BAGNALL: Yeah, thank God. He got across the foredeck using the line to the winches. Bill? D'yer wanna mek a link call?

BILL: Na. This int much. No need.

BAGNALL: Roc?

ROC: Yeah, er…I'd like to put a call through to Maureen.

BILL: Proposal. Ha, ha!

BAGNALL: Yer gerrin wed?

BILL: Maureen.

ROC: Yeah.

BAGNALL: Everyone's going mad to get married nowadays. I'll not say nothing, but you do know you're making a terrible mistake don't you?

ROC: Yeah.

(Silence.)

BAGNALL: What about you Norman?

BILL: Ha, ring yer mother?

NORMAN: Yer what?

BAGNALL: Do you wanna mek a link call?

(NORMAN gets out of his bunk.)

BILL: He'll wanna ring his mammy.

(NORMAN smashes the butterflies that BILL has been making.)

NORMAN: *(Screaming.)* No, no, no, no!

BILL: *(Stands and advances on NORMAN who backs away.)* Yer fucking scummy bastard!

(ROC and BAGNALL leap out of their bunks. ROC gets between BILL and NORMAN and holds NORMAN off.)

ROC: That's alright Bill!

BILL: D'yer see him? He smashed me butterflies!

ROC: Alright. He dint mean it!

BILL: Yes he fucking did mean it!

(BAGNALL backs BILL back into his seat. ROC has a hold of NORMAN from behind. NORMAN is sobbing, and trying to hide it.)

I'll fucking do you! Look at them!

(The two are separated.)

ROC: It's alright Norm. It's alright.

NORMAN: I need a shit.

ROC: Go on then!

(NORMAN leaves to the drying room.)

BAGNALL: You're gonna marry her then?

ROC: Yeah.

BILL: But Norman's fucked her. Ha, ha, ha.

BAGNALL: Tut! Kinnel! What is wrong with that kid?

BILL: Mebbe she's up the duff, have you thought of that? Ha, ha, ha.

ROC: She told me what happened. What he did to her.

(A big sea hits. A loud bang. After a few moments it is clear that the ship is now listing.)

BAGNALL: She's gorra list on.

ROC: Yeah. That's a list. Int it?

BILL: Na, na. She's coming back. Full ahead, come on!

(They stand and will the ship to come back. BILL slips a hand under his pillow and finds his rosary beads. Enter NORMAN, with only his Bowie T-shirt on, ie: no underpants. He is carrying a fresh turd in his right hand. He is sobbing and shaking.)

NORMAN: It's not as warm as I thought it'd be. It went cold real quick.

ROC: Jesus! Come on.

(ROC leads NORMAN out to the drying room.)

BAGNALL: He's not right upstairs is he?

BILL: Upstairs? Downstairs? Kaw!

BAGNALL: But Roc's gonna get wed?

BILL: Oh aye, ho, ho, ho.

BAGNALL: Be good for him. Norman's a terrible bad influence on that poor lad.

(A big wave hits with a bang. BAGNALL and BILL grab on to the furniture.)

Shit! Come on, full ahead, get her back! Full ahead, come on! For fuck's sake, full ahead, come on! She's going Bill, she's going!!

(The engine noise changes as she goes full ahead. She rights herself but with a list.)

BILL: That's it. That's right, there you go.

(The ship now has a significant list.)

See. Told yer. Aye, they're good sea ships these.

BAGNALL: That's a list. She's gorra list on.

BILL: It's onny the wind pushing her down.

(NORMAN and ROC enter. The turd has gone, and his hand is clean. ROC is leading NORMAN with an arm around his shoulder. NORMAN buries his head in ROC's chest. He is whimpering.)

BAGNALL: That's more than a fucking list. We're heeling over. We're going over Bill!

(BAGNALL heads for the companionway.)

(To ROC and NORMAN.) Come on!

(To BILL.) Next big un and we'll be over!

BILL: I'm gonna mek a start on these.

(NORMAN hangs onto ROC still sobbing. BAGNALL exits up the companionway.)

BAGNALL: *(Off.)* Rocco! Rocco!! Come on! She's heeling over! We're going over!

(They are caught in tableau for a few seconds. ROC holding NORMAN, still sobbing, to his chest. BILL sits and picks at his butterflies.)

(To black.)

The Arctic Kestrel

2002. The forecastle of the museum ship, the Arctic Kestrel. The bunk area and table is roped off from the public. The big girlie pin-up is now replaced by a poster of different kinds of fish. On the bulwark just inside the door is attached a cassette player wired to a speaker above. The tape is playing. It is the sound of a ship head to wind and dodging in a strong gale. A reprise of the James Joyce but the sound is much tinnier. It is obviously a loop tape.

Enter DARREL. DARREL is played by the actor who played CASSIDY in The Kingston Jet. He is carrying a museum dummy of a trawlerman. He comes down the companionway correctly, holding the dummy with one hand, feet into the rungs, and one hand on the rail. He does this slowly and carefully, because he has a smashed and rebuilt hip. He is now 54. He is dressed in a V-neck jumper and Terylene slacks, grey shoes, and a bland anorak. On his anorak is a badge declaring ARCTIC KESTREL – CURATOR. The dummy has been created especially to look like a young, 1960s deckie, ie: DA haircut, tattoos, dressed in a vest and Y-fronts. DARREL sits the dummy on the bench on the stage right side of the table. He studies him to see how authentic he looks. He takes out a packet of Silk Cut and puts a cigarette in the dummy's mouth.

DARREL: Champion.

(He puts one cig in his own mouth, thinks, and puts it back in the packet, and sighs. He opens a small, brown, buff envelope and takes out a cassette. He stops the loop tape cassette playing and replaces it with the new cassette. He presses play. The new cassette has the same head to wind and dodging sound as before, but has audio narration over. It is not DARREL's voice, but it is a strong Hull accent, and obviously an ex-trawlerman.)

NARRATOR: 'You're now standing in the forecastle of the Arctic Kestrel and it's in 'ere under the whaleback –

(DARREL leaves up the companionway.)

– where the crew's quarters was situated in the steam powered sidewinder trawlers which worked the distant water grounds of the arctic circle. Theirs were simple pleasures, cigarettes, cowboy novels, and o' course, story telling –

(DARREL enters carrying a second dummy, which he positions on the bench.)

Everybody had a tale to tell about Arthur Duggleby, Cassidy as he was known, you'lla seen his statue on dockside in front of the museum. Cassidy epitomised the spirit, bravery, and sense of humour of these hard worki–

(DARREL switches off the tape. He arranges the second dummy and puts a cig in the dummy's mouth. Enter PAT, carrying a third dummy. PAT is played by the actor who played NORMAN in the James Joyce. He comes down with heels into the rungs facing forward. He is 29 years old, and small, about 5' 6". He has a hyperactive, fidgety manner. He wears casual clothes, cheap market stall copies of named brands. He has a pierced ear. He carries a bag, like a newspaper boy's bag, slung across his chest. DARREL stands.)

DARREL: Hello?

PAT: Hiya. This is yours innit?

DARREL: Yeah.

PAT: There's some lads hanging about up there.

(DARREL takes it off him and puts it into one of the bunks stage left. PAT gives himself a shot from an asthma inhaler.)

DARREL: We're closed. How d'yer gerr on board? The gate's shut.

PAT: There's one more up on dockside. I'll gerrit in for yer while I'm at it, yeah?

DARREL: No, I'll go. Are you one of the lads what helped with the painting?

PAT: Yeah. D'yer wanna hand?

DARREL: No, that's last one.

(DARREL exits up the companionway. Quickly, PAT goes beyond the rope, and feels the table, discovering that it is fixed, as he expected. Quickly, he takes out a battery operated nail gun from his bag. He places it carefully on a mattress in one of the bunks behind him. He goes into his bag again and takes out a second nail gun. He puts it carefully on the bunk next to the other one. He then gets back behind the public's side of the museum rope. He is edgy, and looks around. He puts his bag down against the bulwark. He presses the tape and listens.)

NARRATOR: – men. My favourite Cassidy story is the time he was in Wilson's butchers shop when this old dear comes in and buys a rabbit for her Christmas dinner and Cass wan't having that so he bought her two turkeys, and then the word goes up –

(DARREL enters with the last dummy.)

'Cass is buying turkeys' –

PAT: (*Simultaneously.*) Cass is buying turkeys!

NARRATOR: – and he spends all day in there buying turkeys for anyone who pleads poverty. Ha, ha, ha, a funny story, and –

(DARREL turns the tape off. DARREL places the dummy in one of the bunks downstage left.)

DARREL: Couldn't see no-one.

PAT: Do you mind if I smoke?

DARREL: No smoking in here.

PAT: (*Pointing to a dummy.*) He's smoking.

DARREL: Huh. I'm locking up now.

(PAT goes into his bag and hauls out a huge duty free box of cigarettes. He takes a box of twenty out of the bigger box, takes a cig for himself, but does not light it. He offers one to DARREL.)

(*Assertively.*) I said, it's no smoking in here son.

PAT: What school was that? The girls?

DARREL: Fifth form. Newlands High.

PAT: Me Uncle Ted ses that Hull is a divided city. East Hull's Christian and West Hull's pagan. Do you think any of them lasses were pagans?

DARREL: Why don't you go and ask them?

PAT: I'm already in a love triangle.

DARREL: We're closed.

PAT: I've bin round a mine museum near Donny wi school. Your missus took us round.

DARREL: You're one of hers are yer? Mally Lambert eh?

PAT: Was, aye. 'Two dogs' we used to call her.

DARREL: I won't ask. Come on. I'm off now.

PAT: Darrel Ascough.

DARREL: That's me name yeah.

PAT: Darrel. That's a lass's name in't it?

DARREL: Yes.

(PAT holds out his hand to shake.)

PAT: Pat. Or Ciggies Pat.

(DARREL declines to shake hands, instead he bends down, with some difficulty because of his hip, and picks up PAT's bag.)

DARREL: Here's yer bag, Pat. Offski.

PAT: Do you know how Adolf Hitler used to bend down?

DARREL: Do I know how Adolf Hitler used to bend down?

PAT: Yeah. He invented kinetic bending.

(PAT drops his lighter on the floor. Then bends down kinetically and picks up the lighter.)

Like that. Keep your back straight, bend yer legs. Meks you think dunnit. There was no need for the Third Reich he would've found immortality on the basis of kinetic bending alone.

DARREL: Is that what our lass taught you at school?

PAT: I liked her but she taught me nowt. This museum's crap an' all.

Everybody knows about Cassidy already, and all that fucking fishing stuff –

DARREL: – and what did you learn about coal mining?

PAT: You're not allowed to smoke.

DARREL: What do you want Pat?

PAT: Yer knew me dad.

DARREL: Oh aye. Shipmate?

PAT: Yeah. He's dead.

DARREL: He's one of them that died is he?

PAT: Yeah. Frank Rocco.

DARREL: You're Roc's lad then?

PAT: Yeah.

(PAT lights his cigarette.)

Why'd yer call him Roc?

DARREL: Rocco. Roc.

PAT: Right!

DARREL: I dint know he even had a son.

PAT: I'm a bastard – knoworrimean. My name's Sewell.

DARREL: I'm sorry son. A lot of them did die.

PAT: I don't know owt about Frank Rocco. Have you gorr an ash tray?

DARREL: Here. Sit down.

(DARREL waves him into the seating area. PAT takes a seat and uses the ash tray on the table.)

PAT: Do you wanna ciggie?

DARREL: I'm giving up.

(He offers DARREL a cigarette. DARREL takes one. PAT lights it for him.)

Sorry I was a bit short with yer son, I didn't know you was Roc's lad. We get kids in here sometimes doing drugs, and that. Filthy buggers.

PAT: It's alright in here innit? Is it real or is it plaggy?

DARREL: Better not be plastic. Did me last trip in this. Bear Island. 1975.

PAT: Yer not bin fishing since?

DARREL: No. Ant worked neither, not till this. I went down the joke shop every Tuesday for twenty-five year but they never had no jobs. What do you expect? We don't even run our own country any more do we.

PAT: Me Uncle Ted ses you all got thousands in compensation.

DARREL: I 'ant had a penny yet. I might tell 'em I'm a farmer. Gerra million quid next day then don't yer.

PAT: You sound bitter.

DARREL: Two pints of bitter.

PAT: *(Laughs. Beat.)* What were he like?

DARREL: Roc? He was a real big man.

PAT: Big hearted eh?

DARREL: He was that yeah, but he was six foot four an' all.

(PAT takes a packet of 20 Silk Cuts out of his bag and gives them to DARREL.)

PAT: Tek 'em. Ciggies Pat. This is my vocation. I import ciggies.

DARREL: A smuggler eh?

PAT: Call it an introductory offer. Welcome to my world.

DARREL: No obligation?

PAT: No obligation. Me Uncle Ted ses this Frank Rocco, Roc, got in the raft.

DARREL: Yeah. Me, Roc, and Norman Bamforth.

PAT: This Norman Bamforth, he died straight away, yeah. Me dad lived for four or five hours, yeah? And you lived for another three days?

DARREL: I'm still alive.

(Pause.)

PAT: Have you ever purchased cigarettes on the grey market before?

(PAT takes out his mobile phone and starts entering data.)

DARREL: Yeah, big girl, goes in Rayners, ring in her nose.

PAT: Stella. She's had ear grommets fitted. Difference between me and Stella is that I can hear what you say. She's off to Bolton Art College an' all. Does sculptures out of lard. Melinda Messenger, Frankie Detori, Jesus Christ. She puts them on show under lights and they melt. It's a metaphor innit.

DARREL: Our lass wants me to give up fags.

PAT: How d'yer get off with her? I mean, she's poshish in't she, a teacher, and you, well, no offence but you're dead Hessle Road, aren't yer?

DARREL: Marfleet's ships was all named after writers. The Jane Austen, The George Elliot, The Charles Dickens. I always made a point of reading whoever I was sailing in. Aye, I enjoyed 'em all, except for one bad winter in the Virginia Woolf. When it all finished, I did nowt for ten years cept get divorced. Then I went to a night class – 'Irish literature'. I'd done four years on the James Joyce, so I was kinda on a different level straight away. Our lass was running the group.

(*Beat.*) What's your mother's name? Remind me.

PAT: Maureen.

DARREL: Ah yes, Maureen. I have a shot of rum about this time. Alright?

PAT: Sweet.

(*DARREL stands, PAT stands to protect the nail guns from view.*)

I'll get it. In here?

DARREL: Yeah.

(*PAT opens the locker and takes out a quart of red rum and two tot glasses. He gives it to DARREL. They sit down and DARREL pours, and PAT takes another shot of his asthma inhaler.*)

This was all a long time ago Pat, I mean, why are you...

PAT: Me mam's shagging this bloke on the Gower peninsula. He's got a JCB. She's easily impressed. She left me dad this week and has gone to live in Wales. Me Uncle Ted come round, her brother. He tells me all this about this Frank Rocco. I think I believe him. He's an AA man.

DARREL: These things...yer mam, Maureen...what...what did she have to say about Roc and Norman, and that time?

PAT: She were courting Roc, and then his ship sank. I've never thought me dad was me dad. Psychologically, in my opinion, he's a mental cretin. So genetically, you know... unlikely.

DARREL: Roc was six foot four.

PAT: What'yer saying?

DARREL: Nowt.

PAT: Me Uncle Ted ses you survived cos you had dry clothes on.

DARREL: I was wearing a survival suit over dry clothes.

PAT: Me Uncle Ted –

DARREL: Has this uncle Ted of yours ever been to sea?

PAT: No. He was with National Breakdown for ten years, and then the RAC for a month. They sacked him for tekking money for fan belts.

(Beat.) He ses that Frank Rocco and this mate of his were naked in the raft.

DARREL: Yeah, they were.

PAT: Why didn't you, like, take off some of your dry clothes... off, and you know, share them out?

DARREL: Because then, I would have died.

(Silence. PAT stands and walks around. He takes his mobile phone out.)

PAT: Phone number, brand preference, second choice – never needed, don't worry about that.

DARREL: 5 0 9 7 11. Silk Cut.

PAT: 0 1 4 8 2 – 5 0 9 7 11. Silk Cut.

(DARREL pours himself another drink.)

DARREL: I couldn't go in pubs for a long time after that. I thought I knew what people were thinking. 'That's Darrel Ascough, he was in the raft when Roc and Norman died, and he didn't die, and there's gorra be summat dodgy about that, an't there?' The lads at sea, they understand. But it's all the rest of Hull innit, the know it alls, them who get seasick on Picky Park boating lake. AA men. How I let them die and did nowt. Pat, trust me, Roc and Norman, they went fishing, distant water, and they din't come back, and there in't nowt original about that.

(*Beat.*) Did yer see that plaque on the dock side? Tother side of the Cassidy statue. There's more than enough names up there.

PAT: I'm in a rock band. I play the computer. The band's called 'Cassidy'. Our Stevie, plays the drums. Cass is the only good thing that's ever come out of Hull. William Wilberforce – I'm not black am I, it don't move me; Amy Johnson – a woman; the Housemartins – students, communists, and not from Hull. But Cassidy, well, it's like if you're born in Nottingham it's gonna have to be Robin Hood in't it. I like the Cassidy war stories.

DARREL: Huh. Mekking the firing squad laugh?

PAT: Yeah. Tied up against a barrel, and they let him off, cos he could blow fag smoke through his ears. Do you think that's true?

DARREL: He could do it.

PAT: Yer knew him?!

DARREL: Yeah.

PAT: Cool. I'm impressed.

(*Beat.*) I'm twennie-nine and I've never seen a dead body. Cept on telly. What's it like?

DARREL: I kept expecting them to sit up and say summat.

PAT: Three days. With two naked, dead bodies.

DARREL: Aye, it weren't pleasant.

PAT: Someone's bought Napoleon's cock and balls you know. They're pickled. A hundred and forty thousand pounds.

(*Beat.*) Nicotine patches are cheaper in Belgium – d'yer want me to get yer a couple of hundred?

DARREL: Alright. Do you go to Belgium a lot?

PAT: Once a week. Big Fat Dave's. Did you know that the most popular hand rolling tobacco in Britain's prisons in 1999 was Drum? And it didn't even have a licence for sale until the year 2000.

DARREL: You're making money then?

PAT: I still sign on. Everyone's doing it you see. Lorry drivers, any old scab. Kurds, Albanians, street selling. Fucks me off that does.

(*Indicating the dummies.*) They should be playing cards.

DARREL: Aye, we played a lot of canasta.

(*PAT takes out a pack of cards from his bag. Shuffles them and offers them to DARREL.*)

PAT: Quick trick. Pick a card.

DARREL: Come on son, I've gorra go home now.

PAT: Pick a card. Look at it, and remember it.

(*DARREL takes a card and looks at it.*)

Now purr it face down on the table and put yer hand flat on top. I'm gonna suck the information up through yer hand.

(*PAT places his hand on top of DARREL's.*)

Relax. I'm not gonna get me knob out. We live in an information age Daz. This is one of our kid's tricks. Eh, up, I can feel it, summat's happening. Queen of Hearts!

(DARREL turns the card over it's the Queen of Hearts.)

DARREL: *(Genuinely impressed.)* Ha! Brilliant! That was good! How d'yer do that then?

PAT: Magic.

DARREL: That was very good.

PAT: Ta.

(PAT shuffles the cards.)

I don't know what he looked like, this Frank Rocco, me dad. Mediterranean they say.

DARREL: Roc wan't unlike him, but much bigger. Norman was…

PAT: – Fuck Norman. Bit like him then?

DARREL: Wa…a bit. But you know, I mean, it's nothing like him either really.

PAT: *(Frustrated.)* Tut! Fuck!

DARREL: If you go in the drying room there's –

PAT: – I'm sorry, man! I'm out of order! Scary.

(PAT takes a swig of rum straight from the bottle. PAT stands and paces.)

DARREL: I'd berrer get back. Our lass'll be home now.

PAT: Got another trick.

DARREL: It's gone five Pat.

(PAT still standing, picks up the cards. During the next PAT is standing.)

PAT: Choose another card. Last one, it's afuckingmazing this one. You seen Penn and Teller? Nowt! This is another one of our Stevie's.

DARREL: Last one.

(DARREL takes a card.)

PAT: Look at it, remember it, and put it under the thumb of your left hand, on the table, that's right. Spread your hand out.

(DARREL does as he says.)

Now, tek another card. Under your other thumb. Good. Did you remember them?

(DARREL does the same with the second card.)

DARREL: Yeah.

PAT: It's called the cold thumb trick this. Always works, it can't be explained. Now, shut yer eyes.

DARREL: Oh fucking hell.

PAT: Dunt work otherwise! It won't tek a sec.

DARREL: *(Resignedly.)* Shut me eyes.

(DARREL shuts his eyes.)

PAT: Right, keep them shut. Shut tight. Alright?

(PAT stands carefully, trying not to make a noise, swings around and reaches into the bunks, carefully picking up the two nail guns.)

Can you feel the temperature changing, on the skin of yer hands?

DARREL: No. There's nowt happening.

(PAT is now standing before the table, hiding the guns behind his back.)

PAT: OK keep yer eyes closed. Now tell me what yer cards were. I'm gonna swap them over.

(During the next PAT lowers the heads of the nail guns onto the webbing between Darrel's thumbs and fingers.)

DARREL: Nine of diamonds under the left and King of Spades.

PAT: Nine of diamonds and King of Spades. Remember keep yer eyes closed. Is it gerrin colder?

DARREL: Ha, I can feel something, now, bloody hell –

PAT: Keep your eyes shut, it's working!

DARREL: It's gone cold! It's like –

(PAT fires the nail guns simultaneously. Nails are driven through both of Darrel's hands into the table. DARREL stands and screams.)

Aaaaaaaaagggggghh! Agh! Agh!

PAT: *(Interspersed by Darrel's moaning.)* Oh fuck it worked!

Jesus, bloody hell!

Alright, alright!

Shutup will yer!

Yer not gonna die!

(PAT backs off still holding the guns, slightly amazed that it has worked so smoothly. PAT rushes up the companionway and closes the door at the top. He leaves the nail guns on the table. He snatches the rum, and swigs it. He paces. He gives himself a shot of asthma inhaler. DARREL continues to give voice to the pain. PAT is also extremely agitated, and nervous. DARREL screams, stands, moans, and groans, but is helpless to do anything. The following speech is spread over this period.)

Shutup!

Shutup will yer!

For fuck's sake.

It's not a main vein there you know.

Jesus. Knock it on the head will yer.

If you'd stay still, and stop riving about, it wouldn't hurt so much. I mean, that's the fucking idea any road innit.

You're supposed to be a bloody hard case.

Big hairy arsed deckie.

Jesus, look at yer.

Like a fucking kid.

That's a clean shot that one. Pair of clean shots. You're lucky.

DARREL: (*A quiet moan.*) Ohhhhhh. Jesus!

PAT: All them Roman bicycle thieves, shop lifters and sons of Gods woulda bin nailed through the arm above the wrist. You see, there's no cross bones in the hand is there? You'd just fall off yer perch.

DARREL: Get a doctor!

PAT: You'll get used to it in a minute.

DARREL: I will never get used to this!

PAT: You're talking already. Mekking sense.

DARREL: Come on son. It's fucking killing me this!

PAT: Fost off, yer go white, yeah, you've gone a bit white, good, and if you don't faint at that point then you're alright.

DARREL: Gerr an ambulance! Jesus Christ! Aaaaagh. Jesus!

PAT: Yer not gonna die!

(PAT goes in his bag and takes out a pair of safety glasses. He puts them on.)

PAT: Shoulda bin wearing these. I've ruined your table. Mmm. Our Stevie'll bite a bird's arse just to start a fight. He never does it on a Thursday night cos he goes to his night class. Pet care. Hull's top of the violent crime league you know. Champeeeyons! One person can mek a difference. Cantona.

DARREL: Ring an ambulance son, come on!

(PAT shows DARREL a photo.)

PAT: If I was running this country I'd mek it illegal to tattoo anyone above the neck. You don't see many Kurds selling tabs any more. That's our Stevie. Muscle. But he's been banged up again. He's gonna get the tabs organised on the inside. If I can supply Full Sutton, Hull and Armley with Drum and Samson, I'll be well made up. He said he's gonna take the business off me when he comes out if I don't shape up.

DARREL: I've got nowt to do with your bloody business!

PAT: *(Manic.)* Fucking Kurds! Why does Hull gerrem?! We gorra lorra shit housing they can have. They've all got cars, mobile phones, money for clubbing. Hard-ons while they're dancing. Never seen a pair of tits before. All their women are bagged up all the time.

Mecca is nowt burra distant memory. Hull, this is paradise. Has the pain worn off yet?

DARREL: Don't be fucking stupid!

PAT: Now if the Kurds were to send us a boat load of their best talent, six hundred single girls, that'd be different! But Hull would never get them, oh no. Islington.

DARREL: What do you want son?

(Pause.)

PAT: Eddie Stobbart fell off a roof when he was ten, woke up with a stutter. Problem. On the phone people used to offer him big, difficult, haulage contracts, but he only had one lorry, but because of his stutter he couldn't quibble, he'd just say 'N...n...n... OK!' A problem turns into an opportunity. My problem, Stevie's inside. Opportunity to show that I can look after myself, not be fucked around.

DARREL: I've got nowt to do with your ciggies!

PAT: You killed my father!

DARREL: It wan't like that son!

PAT: (*Manic.*) Don't fucking patronise me! I want some respect here.

This place, that's what it's about isn't it, about how we're shit, and you're I dunno...men...brave, and we're...ah forget it!

(DARREL continues moaning. PAT takes a shot of rum.)

I don't do puff, speed, crack, H, nowt. I'm clean. I'm off the Ritalin. At school I was ADD which ain't as bad as ADHD. I never sniffed glue. I bought the glue cheap, and I sold it expensive. I'm an entrepreneur.

DARREL: Everyone gets a fair crack of the whip with me son!

(*Beat.*) There's gonna be a lot of people about soon. There's two new ships coming in on the tide. Big stern freezers. And our lass is expecting me home.

PAT: I'll ring her.

(He looks at his mobile.)

No reception.

(PAT exits up the companionway. During the next DARREL stands and tries to prise the nails out with his teeth. He fails. He gets blood on his mouth. Pat's footsteps can be heard on the whaleback but not his voice. After a while PAT returns.)

(*Singing.*) Like chicken tonight, like chicken tonight! Guess what's for tea Daz.

(*Singing and doing a chicken impression.*) Like chicken tonight,
like chicken tonight. She said she'd keep it warm for yer.
Like chicken tonight! Go on! Guess what's for tea!

DARREL: Stop fucking about will yer!

PAT: Guess what's for tea!!

(*PAT picks up a nail gun.*)

DARREL: Chicken.

PAT: You've got blood on yer mouth Daz.

(*PAT puts the nail gun down. PAT paces.*)

DARREL: I tried to pull the nails out. I've got false teeth.

PAT: I liked old two dogs. Big tits. I respect women. You
godda nowadays ant yer, or you'd never get yer leg
over. Catherine, she's a blonde, works for Reckitts, she's
a chargehand on the Mr Sheen line. She's six foot two.
I told her that I'd definitely marry her if she got herself
shortened. They take two inches off each leg. Private
operation. Estonia. Melanie. She used to work in Hull
parks and gardens, but then she shagged the Lord Mayor
and now she works indoors in his office. Yup, she's a
mayor fucker. You wimme?

DARREL: I'm listening.

PAT: Emma works on one of them big pig farms near
Withernsea. She dunt have any person to person contact
with the pigs, she's more on the Public Relations side. She
eats too many pork chops for my liking. Whadyerthink
about marriage?

DARREL: Family's all there is. I should know. I've got two of
them.

PAT: (*Laughing.*) See, you're cracking jokes now.

DARREL: Are you gonna kill me?

(*PAT sits opposite DARREL.*)

PAT: I might have to. I'm having a difficult week. Me Uncle Ted ses you killed my father, and you've been lying about it for thirty years. The truth, that's all I want. Why were they naked?

DARREL: Norman and Roc, they were below...when it heeled over. I was on deck. You don't wear deck gear below.

PAT: (*Pointing to a dummy in vest and underpants.*) He's below. He's got clothes on.

DARREL: He wouldn't be wearing that much.

PAT: This museum's not realistic then is it?! Like I said crap!

DARREL: They took their wet gear off in the raft. Wet gear's worse than nowt at all. Norman doesn't last long, ten, fifteen minutes mebbe. He was as good as dead in the water.

PAT: I couldn't give a monkey's toss about Norman.

DARREL: Roc isn't so bad but after a couple of hours he starts mumbling. That's when you know they're going.

PAT: What did he talk about?

DARREL: It's just mumble, nothing, he –

PAT: (*Shouting.*) – I never spoke to my father, there was never a word between us, but he spoke to you! Now! I've treated you with respect haven't I Darrel? Eh? So far?!

DARREL: You've nailed my hands to the table.

PAT: Alright, apart from that! I've been reasonable with you haven't I?

DARREL: Yes.

PAT: So, just fucking tell me what he said! Alright?!

(*PAT bangs his fist on the table.*)

DARREL: Agh! Don't bang the table, please!

PAT: Shit, sorry!

DARREL: They mumble! It never meks sense. He mumbled and held on to Norman, and talked to him!

PAT: Norman's dead you lying twat!

DARREL: Roc held him. And talked to him. They was good mates, yer godda remember that.

PAT: Were they – you're telling me they were queers aren't yer?

DARREL: Oh for fuck's sake! They were kids! Younger than you, they were mates, they were dying together. What's the matter with you?!

(PAT stands, and paces.)

PAT: I have no respect for you, or your mates. What you learn going round these crappy museums is that you didn't have to think. You left school, went to sea, no thinking. No decision making.

DARREL: No son, you're wrong, you've got –

PAT: Cold, long hours on deck?! Fucking bollocks. You had it on a plate pal. No thinking, no decisions, no…no… thinking, there it is again! It's a definite theme in this situation. The almost total absence of thinking, thought. Eh?

DARREL: There was no choice, you…

PAT: That's my fucking point!

(PAT bangs the table deliberately. DARREL groans.)

That's mental work Darrel.

DARREL: Agh!

PAT: Brain fucking work. I'm alright, me, now sorted out. I
mean I can stand up in any pub, I'm Ciggies Pat, but …
agh, you, you don't know you're fucking born!

DARREL: No, no, no, you got it wrong son, you –

PAT: I'm buzzing! I've gorra pulse in me eyes. Do you ever
gerr a pulse in yer eyes?

DARREL: No.

PAT: It's bang bang bang in there.

(*Beat.*) My blood sugar's dropping an'all. You got any
biscuits? Fig rolls?

DARREL: Sorry.

PAT: (*Manic.*) Me Uncle Ted he teks the piss, knoworrimean,
cos I'm small, physically small. He's bin winding me up.
He was saying how I was fucked now that Stevie's going
inside. Last week, in our house there's me, Stevie, me
mam, me dad, our Jenny. Jenny's gone off permanent with
me dad, sorry, me step dad, up Orchard Park with his
new sex option. I dunno what's happening. Just me now.
I mean I was gerrin sick of 'em all rowing and that, and I
was gonna move out anyhow, but…fuck, I dunno.

(*Beat, then desperate.*) My dad bollock naked, on one side of
the raft, and you all zipped up and toasty warm! Isn't there
something fucking disgusting about that! You didn't do owt
did you?! You sat there and you watched him die!

DARREL: Yes!

PAT: How does torture work? I mean, how do I know you're
telling the truth?

DARREL: You don't.

PAT: Why didn't Roc have a survival suit?

DARREL: They wan't standard issue. Health and Safety
hadn't been invented back then.

PAT: How come you had one then?

DARREL: Me dad give it me.

PAT: I've given mesen an headache. Have you got any paracetamol?

DARREL: No. Have a drink.

(PAT takes a swig.)

PAT: What would Cassidy have done? What would Cass have done in your situation?!

DARREL: I dunno! I dunno!

PAT: Have you got mates?

DARREL: Yeah.

PAT: I'm gonna have to kill yer then aren't I.

DARREL: There's a photograph in the drying room, I want you to look at, in there. There's one labelled the James Joyce. Everyone sitting round the table, smiling.

PAT: What? The trip you sank.

DARREL: Don't be daft. Go on, have a look.

(PAT stands and goes in the drying room.)

(Raised voice.) You got it?

PAT: (*Off.*) James Joyce?! Yeah.

DARREL: (*Raised voice.*) Roc's in the middle of the picture.

PAT: (*Off.*) Someone's got him in an 'eadlock?!

DARREL: (*Raised voice.*) Yeah, that's the one.

(Pause.)

PAT: (*Off, quietly.*) Who is that?

DARREL: (*Raised voice.*) You what?

PAT: (*Off.*) Who's giving 'im the 'eadlock?

DARREL: (*Raised voice.*) Norman Bamforth.

(PAT returns holding the picture in his hand, looking at it intently.)

I think they both had a thing with your mother, but
Maureen didn't like Norman over much. I liked Norman.
You alright Pat? I say, I liked Norman a lot. He was good
fun. Bit of a bad lad, but relatively harmless.

(PAT returns to the drying room. He is heard to smash the picture.)

Pat!

(PAT enters and goes straight up the companionway and out.)

Pat! Pat! You can't leave me here like this! Pat! Oh Jesus!
PAT!!

(Silence.

Enter PAT. He stands near DARREL.)

PAT: I've rung Infirmary. I said there'd been an accident.

DARREL: Good lad. You alright?

PAT: Dunno.

DARREL: Gimme a shot of that rum.

(PAT sits and feeds him a drink.)

PAT: I want to make an official apology. I've been badly
advised. Me Uncle Ted. He was a prefab baby. He's a bit
chippy. Born in a prefab, still lives in a prefab, you know.

DARREL: It can twist yer mind.

PAT: They offered him a house but, you know what they're
like…

DARREL: They're a breed apart.

PAT: Yeah, me mam ses me Uncle Ted could never get a girl. There'd always be a deckie throwing his money about. Easy to pull was it?

DARREL: Oh aye. Millionaires for a day we were. Three weeks away and three days home. We had summat about us. We'd been out there, and we'd come back. But he's not got a bad job your Uncle Ted. In my experience everyone's always pleased to see an AA man.

PAT: That's how he met me Auntie Barb. Half way down Sully Way she was, when the sub-frame on her Triumph Toledo snapped in half.

DARREL: If some welder, one day, in Coventry had done a better job, they'd never of met.

PAT: Yeah.

(*Beat.*) How do you know, I mean, how does anyone ever know what is the right thing to do?

DARREL: At sea there's rules for everything. You're right, I didn't have to think much.

PAT: Have I lost your respect?

DARREL: Come on Pat I…

PAT: I'm disgusted with myself.

DARREL: I…

PAT: Have I lost your respect?

DARREL: It's not a case of…

(PAT puts his head in his hands.)

PAT: I'm gonna get Stevie out of my life. I'm gonna be a pacifist from now on. I've always been against the death penalty, unless it's for something really serious. I'll stop wearing leather. No animal products. Vegetarian. I'm me! I'm gonna be me from now on! They're our Stevie's nail guns. He does pub decks. He nailed this smackhead to a table once. The kid hardly batted an eyelid. Pain killer innit, heroin. He's been trying to nick Stevie's tools.

DARREL: You can't shut a window round here without trapping someone's fingers.

PAT: But you're coping better than I did. I passed out.

(PAT shows him the scars on his webbing.)

I forgot to feed his iguana.

DARREL: Yeah?

PAT: What do you think Cassidy would have done?

DARREL: He'd have swam to Norway towing the raft behind him. Dunno.

PAT: Can we talk about your mates?

DARREL: Don't worry about it. Just ring an ambulance and…

PAT: It's on its way. I'm gonna go now.

DARREL: Do you wanna know what my favourite Cassidy story is?

PAT: I've heard 'em all.

DARREL: No you an't.

The trip he died I was the Snacker, and before we sailed he'd told me he had summat in a tin in his house. Summat he wanted me to have on account of me being his only son.

PAT: Well why didn't you say! Bloody hell. You're Cass's son!? Bloody hell!

DARREL: You know he died that trip, the only one to die –

PAT: Yeah, yeah, he jumped out the raft and swam back to rescue Jip, his lucky dog.

DARREL: No, no, no. He'd killed Jip in Criterion *before* the trip. He swam back for no good reason. Come down here I guess. Had a lie down. They're not unlike coffins, are they.

PAT: Suicide?

DARREL: Yeah. I went round his house when we got back. There was no-one there. The next door neighbour said they'd taken his lass off to De La Pole.

PAT: The loony bin?

DARREL: Yeah. The neighbour let me in. I took the tin and left. I opened it up when I got home. There was his war medals, and a betting slip. A treble. Jackson's Daughter, Before Thunder, and Big Horse. All ticked.

PAT: Winners.

DARREL: Yeah. There was a map on the back of the ticket, like a treasure island map.

(PAT gives him a drink of rum.)

PAT: Here.

DARREL: There was a cross in a double circle, like a doughnut, and next to the cross a little bridge type drawing. The words 'Newbald' and 'Golf'. I know Newbald, it's a village near Beverley, and there's a golf course there.

(The sound of a ship's horn at a distance. DARREL hears it but PAT is oblivious to it.)

I bought a two and half inch Ordnance Survey map, and it was there, the little bridge thing, a stile. Yeah, they're dead good them big OS maps. If a cow stands still for long enough they'll draw it in. I got the first bus to Beverley.

PAT: Did you gerron the bus with a spade?

DARREL: I bought one when I got there. I found the stile easy enough. The doughnut thing's a circle of bramble briars with a clearing in the middle.

PAT: You hacked your way in. I'm there Daz, I'm with yer.

DARREL: Once inside it's terrible quiet, you know, cos I'm surrounded, no traffic noise, and the only way I can look is up at the sky, and there's a skylark, and it's watching me. And I dig. And I'm scared cos my ear is twitching which is this fear thing I have.

PAT: Did you find owt?

DARREL: Yeah. A trawlerman's oil frock – rolled up. I know there's summat inside but I can't look. I puke up.

PAT: A body?

DARREL: The police identified them as twin boys.

PAT: 'Kinnel!

DARREL: Killed, and buried on the day they were born.

PAT: Bloody hell. How do they know that?

DARREL: Shape of their heads. They get squeezed don't they, babies, on the way out, and then their heads go back into shape, well these poor little buggers dint gerra chance. He must've midwifed them himself. I can't bring mesen to think about it.

PAT: Why'd he kill them?

DARREL: Cos they were boys. Cassidy had three daughters. He let them live. His father had died at sea.

PAT: I knew that.

DARREL: And his grandfather, and his grandfather's father.

PAT: You didn't die at sea.

DARREL: I should've. I was gonna.

PAT: That is one big fuck off 'orrible story Daz. Who knows about that then?

DARREL: You and me.

PAT: Why did you tell me? You didn't have to.

DARREL: I thought it might help.

PAT: Did you get your money? You know, the betting slip.

DARREL: Yeah, two hundred and sixty. He hadn't paid the tax.

PAT: If I was a copper I'd wanna know what you were doing in a bramble bush with a spade.

DARREL: Nicking bluebells.

PAT: Cool.

(A ship's horn, frighteningly near and loud. PAT stands, frightened.)

Wassat?

DARREL: There's two brand new stern trawlers coming in. What's the time?

PAT: (*Looking at his watch.*) Nearly six.

DARREL: Yeah, that's the tide.

(The horn's sound again, loud and close. Footsteps on the whaleback. PAT stands, now getting edgy. PAT is listening to the footsteps now and not to DARREL.)

PAT: Who's that?

ELLY: (*Off and faint.*) Dad! Dad!

PAT: Who's that?

(PAT puts the nail guns away in his sling bag.)

DARREL: Our Elly.

PAT: Your daughter?

DARREL: Yeah.

PAT: Fuck!

(PAT takes a towel and wipes up the blood from the table and finds another towel and covers DARREL's hands with it.)

What you doing? With your hands? Fuck. Help me, will yer?

DARREL: A card trick.

PAT: Course.

(PAT takes the pack of cards. He sticks the Ace of Clubs on Darrel's forehead. Enter ELLY climbing down the companion-way correctly. She is a girl of about 9. She wears a casual top with a large FCUK logo on it. She's carrying a key on a big lump of wood, which she puts on the table. She stands and looks at the the two men sitting stiffly with cards on their foreheads. An ambulance siren sounds, getting nearer during the next.)

ELLY: Dad?

DARREL: Hiya Elly.

ELLY: What you doing?

DARREL: Card tricks. This is a friend of mine Pat.

ELLY: Hiya.

PAT: Hi.

DARREL: What you doing here love?

ELLY: Mam sent me to get yer.

DARREL: I thought I'd stay and see these ships in.

ELLY: They've come through lock already.

DARREL: Have they?

ELLY: *(To PAT.)* Are you a magician?

DARREL: His brother is.

PAT: Would you like to be a magician?

ELLY: No. I'm gonna be a trawler skipper.

PAT: Oooh!

DARREL: Have yer got a new top Elly?

ELLY: Yeah.

DARREL: Very nice. Where d'yer get it?

ELLY: (*Looking at the logo on the top.*) Next.

(*PAT laughs.*)

DARREL: Alright, alright.

ELLY: Mam ses you've gorra come now. She's gonna have a
    right chow at yer you know.

PAT: I'm off.

DARREL: Go on then. I'll be alright. Go on, fuck off.

ELLY: Dad!

DARREL: Don't tell yer mam.

(*To PAT.*) Elly'll stay with me.

(*PAT exits quickly. ELLY sits where PAT had been sitting.*)

ELLY: Have you been drinking?

DARREL: Yeah, we've been drinking, talking, you know,
    about your grandad, and that.

ELLY: Grandad's statue, he's gorra fish in one hand, and
    summat else, I can't work out, in the other.

DARREL: A firework.

ELLY: What's he got a firework for?

DARREL: Your grandad was famous for...you see, back in the
    old days, they used to light fireworks, you know, at night,
    to attract the er...haddock.

(An ambulance siren is heard. DARREL turns his head. The siren is 'under' during the next.)

ELLY: Have you got a card under the towel then?

DARREL: Yeah, two. Ace of Clubs and...

(Pause.)

ELLY: No! The ace of clubs is on your forehead.

DARREL: Is it? Bloody hell, he's done it! That's the trick! Well, half of it. So, er...only one to go then.

ELLY: He's gone with his card.

(PAT enters. He puts a business card in DARREL's pocket.)

PAT: Ciggies.

ELLY: He's giving up.

(PAT gives his playing card to ELLY.)

PAT: Don't look at it. Lick it and stick it on yer head.

(ELLY does as he says.)

If you're gonna play this game properly, you can't move the towel, alright?

ELLY: Alright.

PAT: I'm not gonna change the name of the band.

DARREL: Tell your Uncle Ted from me, he's a bit of a twat.

PAT: Yeah. See ya.

(PAT leaves.)

ELLY: What's my card dad?

DARREL: I'm not supposed to tell you.

(Pause.)

ELLY: Come on dad, let's go and see the ships.

DARREL: There'll be plenty of time to see the ships.

(She does so, and sits down opposite him. He looks at her directly.)

ELLY: There's a card under the towel, yeah?

DARREL: At the moment yeah. The Jack of Hearts. (*Or whatever card is on her head.*)

We wait you see, it's a matter of patience, and er…at some point the card on your head will change into the Jack of Hearts, you won't know but I'm watching. And then er… that's it.

ELLY: That's impossible.

DARREL: (*Matter of fact.*) It's a rigged pack innit.

(The siren sounds close and stops. DARREL turns his head to listen.

Silence.

The ships horns sound very close. ELLY turns her head to listen. DARREL looks at her as she looks towards the sirens.)

(*To black and the End.*)

Distant Water Trawling Glossary

Distant Water the Arctic fishing grounds

Sidewinder the type of trawler which shot and hauled the trawl over the starboard side; usually between 600 tons (gross) and 800 tons (gross) and about 170 foot long; crew of twenty; three week trips, three days at home

Shackles meat stew

Whaleback the curved deck at the bow

Forecastle crew's quarters

Knocking out the blocks separating the two warps ready for hauling

Dodging keeping head to wind in bad weather

The Old Man the skipper (could be as young as twenty-two)

Snacker deckie learner / apprentice trawlerman

Third Hand senior deckhand

Deckie spare hand / deckhand

Rayners trawlerman's favourite pub on Hessle Road

Criterion second favourite pub on Hessle Road, also known as 'Cri'

Lollipop newsagents with a wide selection of top-shelf titles

Sham Four two up, two down house

Greener big wave

Donkey Hose powered water hose

Printed in the USA
CPSIA information can be obtained
at www.ICGtesting.com
LVHW020930171024
794056LV00003B/682